With lots
love to a
Special friend.
Deb

Hopiland Christmas

Other Books by Bob Lonsberry

Baghdad Christmas

A Various Language

Hopiland Christmas

By Bob Lonsberry

CFI
Springville, Utah

ISBN 978-1-59955-069-5

Published by CFI, an imprint of Cedar Fort, Inc., 2373 W. 700 S., Springville, UT, 84663
Distributed by Cedar Fort, Inc., www.cedarfort.com

Library of Congress Cataloging-in-Publication Data

Lonsberry, Bob.
  Hopiland christmas / Bob Lonsberry.
     p. cm.
  ISBN 978-1-59955-069-5 (alk. paper)
  1. Mormon missionaries—Fiction. 2. Hopi Indians—Fiction. 3. Christmas stories. 4. Religious fiction. I. Title.

  PS3612.O55C48 2007
  813.6—dc22
                                           2007018010

Cover design by Nicole Williams
Cover design © 2007 by Lyle Mortimer

Printed in China

10 9 8 7 6 5 4 3 2 1

Printed on acid-free paper

To all who have answered a prophet's call to preach the restored gospel of Jesus Christ.

🌸 Chapter One

The gingerbread house came about the first of December, in a big box Elder Hammon carried back from town to their trailer behind the church. Town was Polacca, at the foot of First Mesa, on the Hopi reservation in northern Arizona. The trailer was three rooms end to end, from the 1950s, put up on cinder blocks, without plumbing and open to the elements through a broken window in the rear. The church was something of an L, with a chapel and a gymnasium and a row of classrooms sticking off one side. Elder Hammon was a nineteen-year-old with one-sixth of his mission behind him.

He'd broken it down into fractions like that. It was pretty simple math, really. He laid his white handbook flat and traced a quarter to make two side-by-side circles on the front page. One circle was one year and the other circle was the other year and each was cut up like a pie into twelve pieces and various milestones were marked.

1

Two months was one-twelfth, three months was one-eighth and, having just shaded in the fourth piece of the pie, one-sixth was now completed. The next big step would be about Valentine's Day when he'd be a quarter way through.

The box wasn't heavy but it was ungainly, and the wind had been blowing pretty good that day, and the two-mile walk back from town had been a chore. Elder Hammon carried it all the way, though Elder Taylor took his backpack and offered to help with the box but Elder Hammon had said no. It wasn't as much work as it was excitement. Here it was, the beginning of December, and he already had a package. A Christmas package probably. And it was from a girl. A girl from his ward at BYU and he couldn't wait to see what was inside. He couldn't wait to open up this piece of home and drink it in. He couldn't wait to, for half a moment, connect with someplace other than this place.

Because a mission is hard. It's lump-in-your-throat, tears-in-your-eyes hard. Anybody who thinks the best two years of your life come easy or free is nuts. Every good thing comes at a cost, and this is the best good thing. This is walking where Jesus walked, this is doing what Jesus did, this is bearing what Jesus bore. And while he doesn't ask his disciples to follow him into the garden or onto the cross, he does ask them to watch and wait and to share in his labors. And that is soul-building hard. And it doesn't let up until the stake president tells you you're released and your mom takes the name tag from your jacket and you go on to the next set of responsibilities.

And something from home is wind in your sails. At least Elder Hammon felt that way as he stepped up into the trailer, set the box on the built-in table against the wall and went to the drawer to get their one sharp knife. As he sliced the tape the kitchen sink was to his left, the door was behind him and Elder Taylor's bed was on his right. His own bed was behind the partition next to the sink and past the foot of his bed behind the double curtain of old blankets was the junk room with the broken window. They had a stash of extra copies of the Book of Mormon back there and some pamphlets and the various leavings of a couple of decades worth of transient missionaries.

"What is that?" Elder Taylor laughed as the box was unfolded open.

"It's a gingerbread house," Elder Hammon answered, a mix of surprise and disappointment in his voice.

"Can we eat it?" Elder Taylor asked.

Inspection showed that they couldn't. It was beautiful and expertly made, but it was not edible. It was just for looks. Walls of hard gingerbread, firm icing stuck like snow to the roof and the base, red and black licorice outlining windows and doors, peppermints and candy canes all around. It was a gingerbread house. A two-story deluxe gingerbread house with an attached garage.

It sat there until the next morning when they needed

the table for companionship study, and Elder Hammon carried it to the junk room and set it on the floor.

That was the day they tracted out Oraibi. Not New Oraibi, Old Oraibi. Off on Third Mesa.

It had troubled Elder Taylor the two months he'd been there. Elder Hammon's trainer had gone home after a month and Elder Taylor had been transferred in and as Elder Hammon had shown him the area he had just never felt good about the situation with Old Oraibi.

Hopiland—the main part of it—is clustered around three mesas. First Mesa is on the east, on the road to Keams Canyon, and Second Mesa is in the middle, near the road to Winslow. Third Mesa, where Oraibi is, is on the west. The road out that way goes to Tuba City eventually. Each mesa is topped with small rock-and-adobe houses typically arranged in lines or around a central plaza. Most of them are centuries old, passed from generation to generation, little rooms with dirt floors and stone walls and log beams and branches for roofs, topped with mud and adobe. They are low and clean, and the people who live in them are usually short and heavy. Scattered through the mesas in the courtyards and next to the houses are kivas, the churches and clubhouses and temples of the Hopi people. The kivas are partially underground with their entrance through the roof, marked by two long white pine trunks which serve as either side of the ladder providing access.

The irony of the Hopi villages is that they look, to modern eyes, like relics of the Stone Age. They are a place out of time, clustered Anasazi dwellings where the people never went away, where they persisted in their existence and their culture. To modern eyes, it would be a shock to learn that there is such a place in America, or such a place in the world. A giant museum diorama or *National Geographic* special where people live and die much as their ancestors have for century upon century. The temptation of that fact is to presume that primitive is somehow inferior, that these are a backward or disadvantaged people. Actually, they are not. The Hopi villages are a monument to arguably the longest-lived and consequently most successful culture ever to inhabit the Americas. When your villages stand for five hundred or a thousand years, when you survive and throw off a conquest, when you endure and adapt to a climate change, you are not weak, you are strong. You are not to be pitied, you are to be admired.

And that is the history of the Hopis. A history of enduring, productive survival and cohesive, successful social structure. In a land of hunger-gatherers, they planted corn and built homes. While their peers of millennia are ruins and relics, they are alive and kicking, having babies and living lives.

And Elder Taylor respected them. But he also loved them. And there was a conflict there. A conflict that coalesced in his mind in that sign outside Old Oraibi. A conflict in which respect and love crowded one another to stand at the front of the line, a conflict in which each day it became more clear that love and respect were not equals and sometimes not even friends.

Old Oraibi stood on top of Third Mesa, while New Oraibi had built up below, near the government school and the Hopi Cultural Center. Old Oraibi was hard-core Hopi, and it had been for more than three hundred years. That was when the Pueblos—from Hopiland through Zuni and Acoma out to the Rio Grande—rose up one night and took back their lives and their land. The Spanish empire of Mexico had come north and enslaved them with steel and gunpowder, and the atrocities built up, with the stealing and the raping and the killing, until the Indians wouldn't take it anymore. And one night while the priests and the conquistadors slept the Pueblo men fell upon them, all across the Southwest in a synchronized attack planned in the kivas and carried from people to people by runners. By morning the Spanish were dead or in terrified retreat. They never successfully returned to Hopiland. The most significant military victory ever claimed by Native Americans against invaders or settlers was won by corn farmers whose culture and disposition were sworn to peace.

That was something Elder Taylor admired. It was something he used as an opportunity to teach about Captain Moroni and consequently about the Book of Mormon and consequently about Christ. "Your people fought for their families and their freedom," Elder Taylor told person after person, "because they have always fought for their families and their freedom." And then he explained about Lehi and the Promised Land and the visit of the Savior and the great civilization and the sad decline and the promise and purpose of the book and the Lord it testifies of.

Elder Hammon had shown him the sign their first day together. Then they had each posed for a picture in front of it and driven back out from the entrance to the village and around the big bend and past New Oraibi to the Sekaquaptewa's house for dinner. It simply said that whites were not allowed. "You don't obey your own laws, why should we trust you to obey ours?" And for as long as anybody could remember, no white people had gone past that sign. Neither had any Latinos or blacks or Polynesians. It was a Hopi-only zone, and everybody respected that.

Elder Hammon accepted it as a matter of course. His trainer had shown him the sign and told him not to go into Old Oraibi and all the members abided by it and it was just the way it was. Which gets back to Elder Taylor's conflict. He was a Mormon boy and sometimes for a Mormon boy things are kind of straight up. There are not a lot of shades of gray and what-ifs. And he was bothered by the notion that he had been called by a prophet of God to preach the gospel in this particular mission and that his mission president had sent him to preach the gospel in this particular area and now some sign on a post was telling him that a certain place and a certain people were off limits. He didn't feel good about it.

So one morning as they sat down at the little built-in

table in their trailer Elder Taylor produced a quote he'd had his father look up and send to him, and a couple of verses of scripture hand-printed in dark, block letters on either side of a three-by-five card. They had prayer and Elder Taylor said that he'd been thinking and he wanted to bounce something off Elder Hammon. So he laid the three-by-five card down, facing Elder Hammon, and he recited aloud the words on it.

"Behold," he said, "I am a disciple of Jesus Christ, the Son of God. I have been called of him to declare his word among his people, that they might have everlasting life."

Then he flipped the card over, with the words again facing Elder Hammon, and he recited the new verse.

"And he said unto them, Go ye into all the world, and preach the gospel to every creature."

He emphasized "all" and "every."

These two verses weren't new to Elder Hammon. He had known them since boyhood and focused on them since his call and probably back at the MTC they'd gone over them a half a dozen times, just like when Elder Taylor went through. But the scriptures are a funny thing, a common man's liahona, and they mean different things and say different things depending on a person's situation. The Spirit works on the faithful mind and gives meaning to often-read words which has never been seen before, because it has never been needed before. And there at the little built-in table in the elders' trailer behind the Polacca chapel, those verses meant something new and specific.

"Old Oraibi," Elder Hammon said. As the words came out he and Elder Taylor felt a wave of spirit come over them and confirm to them that what he had said was right and true. It was a ratification they tried to build their days around and which they tried to teach their investigators about.

Then Elder Taylor read the quotation he'd had his father send.

"This is from a talk Ezra Taft Benson gave at BYU. He said, 'Stick by your righteous guns and you will bless your fellowman. Be right, and then be easy to live with, if possible—but in that order.'"

For the next half hour they talked back and forth the way people do. Explaining and re-explaining to one another what they'd read and what it meant and how they wanted to proceed. They were disciples of Jesus Christ and they had been sent by him to declare his word to his people. That included the people in Old Oraibi. They were his people as much as anybody else, and maybe even a little bit more, and if they, as missionaries, had been sent by the Lord, then who or what could possibly stand in their way, or cause them to shirk their responsibility? And if the Lord said "Go ye into all the world," that meant every nook and cranny, not just the far-flung lands around the globe, but the corners and pockets of their stewardship and responsibility. All the world includes places across the street as much as it includes places across the sea.

And, no, people probably wouldn't like it if two non-Hopi guys walked past that sign and went door to door talking about Jesus. It probably would cause a stir. It might even cause some hard feelings. It might even be seen as disrespectful to the wishes or the culture of the people of Old Oraibi. But an apostle of the Lord had said to stick to your righteous guns. He'd said to be right and then, if you can, be easy to live with. But the first responsibility is to be right. Far better to have to answer to people for disappointing them than to have to answer to the Lord for disappointing him.

So that morning they pulled out their planners and set a companionship goal to tract out Old Oraibi. To take the priesthood of God and the gospel of Christ to the top of Third Mesa. They fasted about it that Sunday and prayed over a date and on the designated morning, the day after the gingerbread house came, they set out for the drive across Hopiland.

It's a beautiful country of vast, open, arid spaces. Mesas and rocks and a few old cinder cones. Expanses of sage brush and cottonwood washes where the coyotes howl and in the summer the horned toads scamper for shade and supper. As Elder Hammon and Elder Taylor drove they smelled the mildly acrid mix of smoke that hung over the scattered homes. Coal or cedar from the houses and dried sheep manure from the smoldering heaps where the women were firing their pottery. It was a great day to be in Hopiland. It was a great day to be a missionary.

It's a funny thing about being a servant of the Lord. The more faithful you become, the less it's about you and the more it's about him. The less your priorities and fears matter and the more his will and power bear sway. But still they were afraid. That first-day-of-tracting fear that every missionary knows. The what-should-I-say-to-my-neighbor fear that every member knows. The fear that is the fog through which faith alone can pass. They felt that fear as they parked by the sign at the entrance to the village and hesitated for a moment. But it was just a moment, and then Elder Hammon said, "I'll say it," and for a final time they asked the Lord's blessing upon their undertaking.

The walk into Old Oraibi seemed long and they felt self-conscious. They didn't pass anyone but as they came closer to the village they knew people were watching them. Some of the homes were in poor repair, knocked in and abandoned, and the dirt beneath their feet seemed littered with bones and pottery shards, the things of archaeological digs. It seemed unnaturally quiet. Elder Taylor began whistling "Ye Elders of Israel." Elder Hammon pointed to a line of stone houses and said, "Should we start there?" Elder Taylor nodded and they walked to the door, framed by the trunk of a small tree, and knocked on the wood.

"Loloma?" Elder Hammon called. He waited a moment and knocked again. "Loloma?"

There was a light smoke coming out of the pipe in the roof but no one answered the door so Elder Taylor slid off his backpack and unzipped it to retrieve the stack of five-by-seven pictures of Jesus they'd brought. Over the previous mornings they had signed every one of them on the back: "Merry Christmas from the servants of the Lord. He has sent us with a message of peace and joy for your family." Then there were their names and their phone number and the time church met on Sunday. Elder Taylor stuck a picture between the door and the frame and handed half the pile to Elder Hammon.

Four doors and four pictures of Jesus later the first door they had knocked on opened and the picture fluttered to the ground and an arm quickly bent down to retrieve it before the door closed and the house was lifeless again. It happened that way repeatedly. Sometimes when they knocked they heard radios inside or saw people peeking from interior rooms, but for more than an hour no one answered, though after they had passed most of the doors opened and the pictures of Jesus were eagerly taken inside.

In the four hours it took to knock on every door in Old Oraibi, the missionaries spoke to just six people. One was a visiting nurse, four were old grandmothers, and the sixth was a guy who had gotten out of the Marine Corps in the fall and missed it. None of the grandmothers spoke English but all of them seemed kindly. All six took a picture of Jesus. But that was it. They had come into Old Oraibi, they had tracted it out, they had left behind a lot of pictures, they had made some small talk, but all they'd gotten for their efforts was the cold shoulder. Nobody confronted them for coming into the village, but nobody welcomed them either. Mostly they had encountered a ghost town where people didn't answer their door and the few who were out took great pains to stay some distance away.

Until the school bus came.

Just about three o'clock, as they were walking back through the village toward where they'd parked, the missionaries heard the children coming. Laughing, happy children. Running, like children will, full of life and back from a day at school, eager for home and play and dinner. Children who, when they saw the missionaries, became visibly excited and curious. What a sight it was, startling almost. Two strange men, in suits and short hair, walking through the village of stone and adobe atop the dust of centuries.

Some ran to their homes, some nervously hung back, some cautiously approached. The teenagers and the elementary kids, electrified by this unusual sight. It took only moments for some of the children, the ones who had run to their homes, to make the connection between the two men and the pictures of Jesus. Then everybody wanted a picture of Jesus and emboldened by the possibility and the pretext they circled the missionaries and began to ask and beg and tease. Five at first and then a dozen and quickly a couple of dozen and more.

That led to one of those times when the Lord tells

you to zig when you had expected to zag. When the quick whisper of the Spirit changes your course. When the prayer of faith is answered in a moment of unexpected and unseen importance.

"No!" Elder Taylor shouted, raising his hand with the pictures in it high above his head. "No pictures for you. Not until you sing us a song."

"We can't just give these away," Elder Hammon joined in. "You have to earn them. You have to sing us a song. A Christmas song."

Children love to laugh, especially Hopi children, and the teasing about the pictures and the request for a song struck these particular children as comical. They laughed loud, and Elder Hammon had to raise his voice to be heard above them.

"'Silent Night,'" he said. "We want you to sing us 'Silent Night.'"

"Hold it," Elder Taylor said, "don't start yet." He quickly organized the kids into two lines, facing a short wall at the edge of the plaza, and sat himself and his companion on the wall and said, "OK, now you can sing. Ready? OK, start!"

It was a giggly, off-tune rendition, but it was "Silent Night." It started weak and grew strong as the young voices fell into unison and warmed to the task. When a verse was done the missionaries cheered and clapped and shouted, "Do it again!"

That was what broke the ice. When the song was

done the two lines came apart and crowded around the elders as they passed out pictures of Jesus. The children asked about their name tags and who they were and where they were from and what they were doing there. For several minutes it was a comfortable, curious meeting. The children seemed at ease and there was no hostility whatsoever, though the missionaries were certain that people in half the village were straining out their windows to watch what was going on.

"Actually," Elder Taylor said, "we're trying to organize a children's choir. We're having a Christmas party at our church on Christmas Eve, and we need some children to sing. Just a couple of songs. It won't be too hard, but it's only about three weeks away, so we need to get working on it.

"Say, you guys wouldn't want to be in our choir, would you?"

They were making it up as they went along. Or more correctly, the Lord was giving them what they needed as they needed it. The Savior promised his ancient and modern disciples that he would teach them, in the very hour, what to say in a given situation, and in the plaza at Old Oraibi that day he kept that promise.

"Here's what we're going to do," Elder Hammon said, "tomorrow at three when you get home from school, we are going to be here to hold a choir rehearsal. Talk to your families and tell them we want you to sing at our church on Christmas Eve and that they are invited and that we're going to come back here tomorrow for a rehearsal. Is that a deal?"

"OK," Elder Taylor said, "we'd really like to see you tomorrow. But we have to go now. But before we do, we're going to say a prayer. While we pray, everybody has to be very quiet. OK?"

Then he folded his arms and bowed his head and asked the Lord's blessings on the children and their families and the village. The children mostly stared out of curiosity. Some bowed their heads, and others crossed themselves. When he was done his companion said, "Amen," and after passing out some more pictures of Jesus they walked out of the village to their car, escorted by a few of the children. They drove out toward the highway but pulled over and stopped before they got to it to offer a prayer of gratitude.

That night they had dinner with the Landrys behind the Polacca trading post and then went to ask the branch president if they could organize a social for Christmas Eve. Later, just before bed, Elder Hammon went into the junk room in the trailer to get some more pictures of Jesus and noticed that something had been nibbling on his gingerbread house.

"You ever been with Wilson?" Elder Hammon asked Elder Taylor. "I heard he was a psycho."

"Charlie?" Elder Taylor said. "He's a great guy. He's a road-less-traveled guy, but he's the best. I was with him down in St. John's last summer. We were there on the Fourth of July and got up early in the morning to be there when they fired off the cannon. Lot of nice members there. Charlie's a short guy, his tie's always half undone, with a giant smile, everybody's friend."

For as long as anyone still in the mission could remember, there had been a senior-companion bush and a junior-companion bush at the back of the Polacca trailer. One was at one corner and the other was at the other, through the thin metal that separated the junk room from the outdoors. They were sage brush or tumbleweed or something, those round prickly bushes that dot the West and collect up against fences when the spring winds blow. The missionaries had a key to the chapel, and they showered there in the morning, but at night sometimes as they were coming in and it was dark, a half mile from the nearest neighbor, the bushes were put to use, one by the senior companion and the other by the junior companion. The competition was to see which bush would grow the biggest and periodically the elders would come out in the daytime and measure, with one of them boasting of his win at the next district meeting. Elder Taylor gave the height of the biggest bush to the zone leaders each week when they called for stats. Elder Hammon had posed for a picture with his bush one time and sent it to his brother who was an assistant in Argentina.

"Give me a warning," Elder Hammon said. "Tell me who I don't want to be with. Who are the guys in the mission I want to avoid?"

"I don't know," Elder Taylor said. "There are all kinds of guys out here.

"Some of them are different. Some of them will rub you the wrong way. But I always figured probably I rubbed them the wrong way, too. I haven't met a perfect missionary, yet. But I haven't met anybody I couldn't work with either."

"I'd just hate to get with somebody who drove me nuts," Elder Hammon said. "That's the one thing that I'm really afraid of."

"I wouldn't worry about it," Elder Taylor said. "What's going to be is going to be. And I think in life you've got to realize that when the Lord blesses you it isn't always fun. I figure whoever I get put with, it's the Lord's will and he does things for a reason. I might not always understand that reason, but it's always there and I've got to have faith in that. And my obligation is always the same. I've got to work hard, love the people, help my companion and live up to my calling.

"And my companion's got to do the same thing. He and I might be different in certain ways, but we're both missionaries, we're both children of God, we're both members of the Church. I think we can work anything out, we can get through anything. And remember, you're not supposed to endure your companion, you're supposed to uplift him. Maybe the soul you were sent out here to save is your companion. Maybe the soul he was sent out here to save is you. Maybe you're the answer to his parents' prayers. Maybe he's the answer to your parents' prayers."

"Do they teach you this stuff at senior-companion school?" Elder Hammon said.

"No," Elder Taylor said. "The Three Nephites taught me."

"Really?" Elder Hammon said. "I was talking to them the other night and they said they'd never met you."

"If that were true you'd know their names," Elder Taylor said.

"I'll tell Larry, Moe and Curly you said hello," Elder Hammon said.

The desert sky is brilliant at night and the Milky Way stretched above them like a swath of glory from horizon to horizon. The air was dry and crisp in the winter chill, the only lights were along the road to the mesa near the trading post, and in the oblivious pitch stretching behind them a small pack of coyotes was yipping.

"There's no such thing as a bad missionary," Elder Taylor said. "Sure, there will be guys who will mess up an area, and there are guys who aren't as good as they could be. But the worst guy out here put his name on the line and his life on hold. The prophet said every worthy young man should serve a mission, and a guy who obeys that has set himself apart. He's shown me something. That makes him special in my book.

"Nobody knows how long two years is like a nine-teen-year-old, and anybody who comes out is my hero, and I'm going to respect him and his calling. Even if he doesn't. It's a big deal to be a missionary, and I don't say that to boast, but because I believe in it. I believe in the calling."

"Same here," Elder Hammon said. He had turned away from the trailer and was looking out toward where he heard the coyotes, trying to see them in the dark. He had folded his arms across his chest to stay warm. "Sometimes I don't think the members respect us. I think they think we're another part of the priests quorum. I know we're young, I know we haven't lived as much life as they have, but if the Lord trusts us, I wish they would, too."

"Yeah," Elder Taylor said, "I think most of them do. Some of them don't. We've just got to do our part. Obey the rules, set an example, act like representatives of the Savior and eventually they'll treat us like representatives of the Savior. If we respect our calling, they'll respect our calling. 'Ye are the light of the world,' the Savior said, and I think that means all the time. Example, example, example. Work hard, love the members, that's our duty."

"Agreed," Elder Hammon said.

Then he turned and walked along the side of the trailer to the door. Elder Taylor followed him, and they stepped one after another up the stair and inside into the warmth.

※ Chapter Two

Brother Coochyumptewa lived facing the plaza by Snake Rock in Walpi. He and his wife and their little boy lived in a room of rock and adobe furnished with a bed and a table, two chairs and a camp stove. The plaza was narrow and long, no more than twenty feet wide, with one side dropping off the cliff-like edge of the mesa and the other bordered by the pueblo homes, coarse rock cubicles sometimes stacked two or three high. Snake Rock was a stone, ten feet tall or more, a rough shaft that stood in the plaza where for generations before the Snake Dance had been performed. On one side was carved at eye level a slight recess where most of the time a smaller stone sat, a fetish of some sort, a prayer feather tied around it and sometimes sprinkles of blue corn meal. At the edge of the plaza there was a passageway, a covered walk that ran beneath the second level and emerged on the back side of Walpi. To the left of the passageway was a wooden ladder that climbed to the second level. From the top of the ladder a small set of stairs on the left led to Brother Coochyumptewa's door.

The missionaries visited once a week for dinner.

Elder Taylor parked the car at the end of Sichomovi, one of three villages on First Mesa. The road came up the side of the mesa and when it got to the top, Tewa was to the right and Sichomovi was to the left. Where Sichomovi ended the mesa got very narrow, almost like a foot bridge, and led to Walpi, which sat at the end, on a tip of rock with a stunning and panoramic view that extended dramatically in three directions. Some eighty miles away, on the horizon, stood the San Francisco Peaks near Flagstaff.

"I love it up here," Elder Hammon said.

"Me, too," Elder Taylor said.

They got out of the car and walked toward the neck of stone that crossed to Walpi. It was like walking centuries into the past. Walpi was the initial Hopi village on First Mesa and it was ancient, with Sichomovi growing later in more modern form as an expansion village and Tewa given as home to a tribe which allied itself with the Hopi. The Tewa were a separate people who benefited from Hopi prosperity and culture and whose job it was to fight off raiding Utes and Navajos.

Elder Hammon and Elder Taylor had spent most of the day down below, at Polacca, chopping wood and hauling water. For lunch they had split a rotisserie chicken from the trading post and taken a brother back home to his wife. He was a man with a drinking problem and, with no alcohol on the reservation, he had for a time bought Listerine from the trading post, until they caught on to him, and today, with the new girl at the register, he had bought and drunk a bottle of Aqua Velva and he was pretty sick. So they took him home to his wife, and she had them give him a blessing and the rest of the afternoon had been split between doing service in Polacca and going over to Old Oraibi to practice Christmas songs with the kids.

They had come up to Walpi about an hour before Brother Coochyumptewa was expecting them, not to arrive early, but to spend a little bit of time on the end of the mesa, reading their scriptures and enjoying the view.

Besides, this was going to be a big night. They had something to say to Brother Coochyumptewa and they wanted the Spirit with them when they did it. Two days before, the president had driven out to see them and to tell them that the stake president felt impressed to call Brother Coochyumptewa as the new branch president. That's not something missionaries would normally be told about, but this was an unusual situation and both president and the stake president thought the elders could help. And maybe they could. They had made pretty good friends with Brother Coochyumptewa, and he trusted them, and tonight they had to talk to him.

Crossing the neck to Walpi they walked into the village on the right hand side, the north side, to avoid the plaza and Snake Rock and because they wanted to stop at an outhouse, a stone hut that stuck out off the edge of the mesa. There were several along the leeward side and Elder Hammon went into the first one they came to. When he was new in the area, just a week out of the MTC, Sister Navasie had told him the story of how Tewanima died. He had been an Olympian, a great runner, a classmate back at Carlisle of Jim Thorpe, and when he was an old man, in the dark of the night going to an outhouse, he had accidentally walked off the mesa. She had told him the story to frighten him, the new bahanna, and for weeks he had been afraid to use the outhouses on the mesa, for fear he would stumble and fall. That had been a good day, he remembered, as she had taught him and his trainer how to paint designs on pottery with a strand of yucca fiber. She had a shortened and misshapen right index finger, as if it was missing a joint or something, and the smoothness and beauty of not just what she painted but how she painted it was impressive. It was a brown dye on the white-slip pots and a series of lines and curves, something she had learned as a girl and which was visible on the little shards of broken pottery that were all over in the dirt of Old Oraibi. Many of the women were potters and many of the men carved kachina dolls, and on P-Day the elders in the district sometimes gathered clay from the gap in First Mesa and cottonwood roots from the washes between there and Winslow. They gave what they found to people who couldn't get their own, mostly old people and ladies who had small children at home.

Elder Taylor and Elder Hammon walked as far out the point of the mesa as they could. The houses stopped at a certain point and the mesa narrowed to a tiny finger of hard rock. They sat down at the end, the desert floor a couple of hundred feet beneath them, the topography jutting before them in every direction and the San Francisco Peaks on the far horizon, the December sun lowering toward them. Elder Hammon said a prayer, and they bore their testimonies to one another and opened their scriptures on their laps. That morning, in personal study, each had looked for verses that spoke of becoming a new man, of being truly and wholly converted. Together now they reviewed those scriptures.

Their passing through Walpi had drawn some quiet attention, as it always did, and they hadn't been sitting on the rock long before a middle-aged man with a dark spirit walked quickly out of the village toward them. He was coming to see what they were up to. They heard his footfalls on the stone and turned to look at him and greeted him as he neared. He glowered at them, looking down at their books, and put his hands on his hips, inspecting the missionaries silently for a moment. Finally, raising a hand toward the west he pointed at the San Francisco Peaks and sneered angrily, "My gods live in those mountains."

Elder Taylor looked at the peaks and then back up at the man's face and said, "Brother, my God made those mountains. And he made you and me, and he sent his Son to save us all. We are here to teach you that. We are here to teach you about a God who is the master and father of us all."

With that the man muttered something in Hopi and turned quickly and stormed away.

It was an unsettling thing, as confronting anger always is, and partly comical, but the missionaries recognized it as a disruption of the Spirit, an attempt by Satan to throw them off, to send them to their meeting shaken instead of resolute. Satan always tries to stop the cause of truth. They talked about it and read a last couple of scriptures and knelt there on the hard stone and asked again for the Lord's spirit and guidance. Then they walked back into the village, along the south edge of the mesa, past Snake Rock and up the ladder and set of stairs to Brother Coochyumptewa's door.

They knocked and were let in and felt the warmth of the little room. Sister Coochyumptewa was turning fry breads with a fork in a pan of hot oil and Brother Coochyumptewa gestured for the elders to sit in the two chairs. He sat beside the baby, who was in a cradle board on the bed. Brother Coochyumptewa was a stonemason and was learning to be a silversmith. When there was stonework to be done he did that, and when there wasn't he drove over to Oraibi to make Hopi overlay. Bracelets, earrings, watchbands. Whatever they asked him to make. He was essentially an apprentice but had taken quickly to it and had already had some pieces sell at the Hopi Cultural Center and at the trading post in Keams Canyon. He was a quiet man with a dry wit and an open heart. He was well liked and respected and he came from a good family. His smile was natural and easy.

"Have you been reading your scriptures?" Elder Hammon asked him.

"Every day, Elder," Sister Coochyumptewa said.

It was her family's house they lived in. It had been for more generations than anybody knew. Elder Hammon, leafing through a tourist book at the trading post, had found a century-old picture of Snake Rock and the plaza and the Coochyumptewa's door was plainly visible in it, identical to how it looked now. He had bought the book and circled the door in the picture and mailed it home to his parents. He wrote, "A golden family lives here," in the margin.

"She makes me do it," Brother Coochyumptewa said. "Every time she changes the baby, I have to read. She says to either read or change the baby. So I read. I think she gives that baby water just to make me read."

Sister Coochyumptewa giggled and shyly turned away. She was not a member but had been at church every week that Elder Hammon had been there. She taught a Primary class and had a visiting teaching assignment. She wanted to be baptized but she wanted her husband to do it and he said he wasn't ready. He didn't explain, he just said not yet. Sometimes that puzzled and frustrated the missionaries. Not just Brother Coochyumptewa, but most Hopis, probably most Indians, have a casual approach to time and timeliness. There was Mormon standard time and Hopi standard time, and between the two most things started about twenty minutes after they were supposed to.

"How's the kiva?" Elder Taylor asked.

That was the hard question. The hard question that would lead to a challenge. Missionaries are not passive, they are aggressive. They have an objective, they are on a quest. They don't leave well enough alone. And sometimes they have to talk about things that people would probably just as soon not talk about. But a missionary who lets people stay in their comfort zone can't lead them to heaven.

"Good," Brother Coochyumptewa said.

"Did you tell them anything yet?"

"No," Brother Coochyumptewa said. "Not yet. I still haven't decided."

Sister Coochyumptewa forked the last fry bread onto a plate and took the lid off a pot of beans. Brother Coochyumptewa asked Elder Hammon to pray and they ate. The elders sat in the chairs and the Coochyumptewas sat on the edge of the bed. Elder Taylor said it was good fry bread, and Sister Coochyumptewa was pleased.

As they ate, Elder Hammon told the story of a dog in the plaza in Sichomovi. A black reservation dog, an odd mix of genetics with random patches of hairlessness, pretty friendly most of the time. Four days before, the missionaries had sat in the plaza to eat their lunch, and the dog had been sleeping soundly in the sun. The next day when they walked through on the way to the Honie's house, the dog was sleeping in the same spot. The next day, when they helped Brother Lumkena haul water, the dog was still there. Elder Taylor walked up to it and noticed that it wasn't breathing. They took pictures of each other posed like they were preaching to it. The missionaries and the Coochyumptewas laughed and wondered how long the dog would be there.

When they were done, Sister Coochyumptewa took their plates, and the elders turned their chairs to face the bed and Brother Coochyumptewa took the family's paperback Book of Mormon and pocket New Testament down off a shelf and held them on his lap. Elder Taylor asked Brother Coochyumptewa if he would say the prayer and when it was over he thanked him and cleared his throat and began to talk.

"Brother Coochyumptewa, the Lord has called you to a new life. The Lord has called us all to a new life. Before we can start following him we must stop following the world. And we must recognize that the world is all around us, in the customs and pursuits of life, in the small things we do automatically and daily," Elder Taylor said.

"It is not easy to follow the Savior," Elder Hammon said. "It is hard to walk where he has walked. He gives us commandments and standards and asks us to follow them. Strait is the gate and narrow is the way that leads to eternal life, and if we want eternal life, we have to walk the narrow path."

"We have to become a new man," Elder Taylor said. "We have to lay aside the old man. We must be truly converted. That means changed into something different, something different and new."

Then he asked Brother Coochyumptewa to open his New Testament to the book of Matthew, to the Sermon on the Mount, to the first sentence of verse 24 of chapter 6.

"No man can serve two masters," Brother Coochyumptewa read. He was slow and deliberate and his voice had the lilt of those who learn to speak on the reservation. "For either he will hate the one, and love the other; or else he will hold to the one and despise the other."

"But you can't serve two," Elder Taylor said. "A two-headed snake doesn't know where to crawl, and a man who is of two minds will not know how to live. If you ride for the brand, you can only ride for one brand. A man can't have a foot in two worlds."

Then Elder Hammon handed his open Bible to Sister Coochyumptewa and asked her to read verse 33 in the same chapter her husband read from.

"Seek ye first the kingdom of God, and his righteousness; and all these things shall be added unto you," she read.

"This teaches us that our duty is to serve the kingdom of God," Elder Hammon said. "And everything else is secondary. Nothing else is more important than that. First we have to serve God and do what he wants us to do, and if we do that he will work everything else out. But if we get our priorities out of order, and put something above the Lord, we have no such promise. In fact, we will be miserable. We will be miserable and we will fail. We will be doing things Satan's way, not the Lord's way."

Then Elder Taylor took a stand.

"Brother Coochyumptewa, the Lord does not want you to be the kiva chief. The Lord has another work for you. The Lord is calling you to follow him and to lay aside those traditions of your fathers which lead you away from him. Brother Coochyumptewa, in the name of Jesus Christ I tell you that you must turn yourself to the Church and away from the kiva."

That was the issue and the source of the tension that underpinned their meeting and dominated Brother Coochyumptewa's life. He had been asked two weeks previously to become the new kiva chief at Sichomovi, in the kiva by the plaza next to the water tank. It was a great honor, a reflection on his family and himself and the regard and esteem his neighbors had for him. It was his by right and by the free offer of the men who gathered in that kiva. He was to fill the empty position once held by his late uncle. He would be responsible for the dances and songs of the various kachinas that came out of that kiva.

Before long it would be the season of the Bean Dance, and the Soyok Wuhti would lead her band of Nataska and Wiharu and the Heheya Kachin Mana out of the kiva to the homes of the village to terrorize and thrill the children. Kachinas are little dolls carved from wood, and they are grown men dressed in ancient costumes and masks, and they are spirits that live part of the year with the Hopis in their kivas and the rest of the year in the distant San Francisco Peaks. Their appearance at the Powamu was the beginning of their return to the villages after a winter away. The Soyok Wuhti and her band of ogres came twice from the underground kiva. Both visits are to the children, who cower in the their homes while the mother kachina and her ogres chant and sing outside, going from house to house, dragging long saws against the stone buildings and howling for blood.

The Soyok Wuhti angrily demands the children be brought to the door and then gives to the boys a few strands of horsehair or yucca fiber and to the girls a few kernels of blue corn. These are left with the children with the instructions that they are to prepare a feast for the kachinas when they return in three days. The boys are to make snares to catch mice for meat and the girls are to grind the corn to make piki. But three days later, when the kachinas return, the children's work is declared unsatisfactory and the Soyok Wuhti and the Nataska and Wiharu say they will eat the children instead. And so it plays out, with the kachinas grabbing the children by the arms and their parents grabbing them by the feet and the poor children screaming in horror as a tug of war is played out at their family's front door. Finally a ransom is offered and the family brings out food to exchange for their children, food that will be the bounty of a village feast.

When one family's children are ransomed, the kachinas move to the next door and the next family and elsewhere in the village children who have yet to be visited quake in fear as the racket and clamor slowly works its way to their home.

This, and the rest of the year's kachina ceremonies, were to be Brother Coochyumptewa's responsibility. He was to teach this and enforce this and pass this on. He was to be chief of the kiva. He was to be the Soyok Wuhti. He was to be the keeper of the faith.

It's like the Santa Claus and the Easter Bunny of the Hopi, except that it's not. It's not a mere cultural expression, a custom, it is a belief, a religious faith, a heartfelt understanding of the eternal and the divine. The Hopis are the people of a family of gods who visit them each year in costumes worn by men, in dances and songs remembered and recited for centuries. The kachinas are a religion, a competing and mutually exclusive religion. And either God died on the cross in Jerusalem or he lives as a spirit in the mountains by Flagstaff, but it can't be both. If deities climb with rattles and feathers from the kivas of Hopiland, then they didn't appear to Joseph Smith in the Sacred Grove. Either God asks us to have faith in his Son, or he expects us to honor him with carvings of wood. But it cannot be both.

And that is the point the elders were trying to make. Not just in specific regard to the traditions of the Hopi, but in general application to the faith of all. There is one

Lord, one faith, one baptism, and that is not just in reference to competing denominations, it applies to the fidelity the Savior demands of all who would take his name upon themselves. God is not the author of confusion, and his house is a house of order, and there is one right way and every other way is wrong. The call of the Christian is to be humble and faithful enough to recognize that and to make the personal sacrifice of self necessary to live it. The lesson of the First Vision is that the heavens have opened and the Lord has declared that the traditions and religions and priorities of men have gone woefully astray.

"Brother Coochyumptewa, the Lord who gave his life for us requires us to give our lives to him," Elder Taylor said. "The Lord said that the man who would save his life will lose it, and the man who would lose his life for the gospel's sake will save it. That doesn't mean lose our life as to the physical body—it doesn't mean we have to die to please the Lord—but it does mean we have to give up our old selves to have a life with Christ.

"Jesus said that you don't put new wine in old bottles. Do you know what that means? He said that if you put new wine in an old bottle, the bottle will break and you will lose both the bottle and the wine. All will be lost. He said that new wine must be put in a new bottle.

"Brother Coochyumptewa, I believe the new wine is the gospel of Jesus Christ. I believe we who accept that gospel are the bottles. I believe that the Lord warned us that to successfully accept the gospel we must become new bottles. If we continue to live our old lives, be our old selves, cling to our old weaknesses and priorities, the gospel will break those lives by showing us the weakness and meaninglessness of them. If we continue to live our old lives, be our old selves, the gospel will not stay with us. It will go away and be lost, and we will be broken and be worse off than when we started. But if we accept the gospel as new bottles, as people willing to be born again and to lay our old selves on the altar of sacrifice, the gospel will be in us like new wine in a new bottle. We will be perfect together. We will be a new creation.

"That is true for every single person who would follow Christ. It's as true for people in my hometown as it is for people in your hometown. All of us are camels that must pass through the eye of a needle, we must be stripped of all that is unworthy and worldly. The Lord has laid before you one course and the kiva has laid before you another. 'Choose ye this day whom ye will serve,' the Bible says, and for you that choice is clearer than for most. But for all the choice is the same. Who's on the Lord's side, who? Will it be you, Brother Coochyumptewa? Will it be me? We each have to decide, we each have to pay the price of that decision. We each have to take a stand."

Sister Coochyumptewa was quietly crying. Her husband was staring at his feet. There was a moment of silence.

"Brother Coochyumptewa," Elder Hammon said. "We are having a Christmas Eve program at the church.

We would like you to come and to give a talk. Some children from Oraibi will sing, Brother Funk will tell the Christmas story, then we'd like you to be the concluding speaker. The stake president will be there, and after the program he would like to meet with you. He has something important he wants to talk to you about.

"Will you do it?"

Brother Coochyumptewa continued to stare at his feet. His wife looked over at him and wiped a tear from her cheek. There was a moment of silence.

Christmas was about two weeks away. That was time enough to make a decision. Maybe too much time. But it was what it was and it was what Brother Coochyumptewa had.

"Let's leave it like this," Elder Taylor said. "You let us know. We will save you space in the program, you will be the speaker, and if you can do it, do it. If you can't, don't. We will be there and the program will be there and the stake president will be there, and we all want you there. But it's up to you. Is that fair?"

"Yes," Brother Coochyumptewa said. "That's pretty good, alright."

And he stuck out his hand. It was a limp shake, but he shook both elders' hands in turn and then Elder Taylor said they should be leaving and who would Brother Coochyumptewa like to say the prayer.

He selected Elder Taylor, and the two missionaries and Brother and Sister Coochyumptewa knelt down in the space between the bed and the table and bowed their heads and closed their eyes.

And that's when the evil spirit hit him. It had happened once before, at Window Rock at a conference when they'd stayed in the old seminary teacher's quarters across from a tipi where the Peyote people had chanted through the night. He had awakened when he heard footfalls on the roof, and then it had seized upon him. Just as it was doing now. A suffocating blackness that tensed his body and choked his breath and left him with the sense that he was drowning, that he was being crushed, that he was surrounded by evil, that he was fighting for his life. He felt the blood pressure go up in his head and he couldn't talk and he couldn't move and with all the force of his spirit he struggled to continue to be.

Perhaps that's what the War in Heaven was like. Perhaps sometimes in mortality it is fought some more. Perhaps the clash of spirit versus spirit is sometimes this gruesome wrestle. Perhaps this is what Joseph felt in the grove. Perhaps sometimes he who would have forced us to be good uses force to fight against the good. And maybe when you strike a blow against Satan it just plain ticks him off and he tries to destroy you.

"In the name of Jesus Christ," Elder Taylor screamed in his mind. "In the name of Jesus Christ I command you to leave." All was dark around him. He was unaware of the other three kneeling near him. He struggled to breathe and to move. He felt as if he was about to be destroyed. "In the name of Jesus Christ of Nazareth, the

Savior of the world, I command you to leave. By virtue of the Melchizedek Priesthood and as a servant of the Son of God I command you to leave this house."

Then his prayer was joined, and without his knowing the hands of a nineteen-year-old surfer from California were placed on his head.

"Elder Archibald Gardner Taylor, as a bearer of the holy Melchizedek Priesthood and in the name of Jesus Christ, I bless you to be free of this demon. As a servant of Jesus Christ I command this evil spirit to depart from you and from this home," Elder Hammon's voice paused. "Mighty is the Lord, Elder Taylor, and invincible, his cause. He will fight the battles of his servants, and uphold their works. He will bless you and this home, and there will yet be great good from both. I bless you with strength, with courage and with freedom from this foe which binds you down. I say this with authority and faith, and in the sacred name of Jesus Christ. Amen."

Elder Taylor gasped and took a series of winded breaths. His body relaxed and the evil was gone and he felt flush and safe. Without unfolding his arms or raising his head he said a brief, silent prayer of gratitude and then spoke a vocal prayer to end their visit. He asked Heavenly Father to watch over the Coochyumptewas in all they did, and to bless Brother Coochyumptewa with faith, wisdom and courage as he made the decision that was before him. Then it was done and they shook hands again and the missionaries walked out into the cool night, down the two steps and over to and down the ladder to the plaza by Snake Rock. In the dark they walked along the south edge of Walpi to the narrow neck and across to the spot where they had parked.

"Satan always tries to stop the cause of truth," Elder Hammon said as he unlocked the driver's door.

"Amen to that," Elder Taylor said. "And he doesn't fight fair."

"Tampiqueña," Elder Hammon said, "with extra sauce, please. Medium rare. And a lemonade. And extra rolls, please. And we're going to want pie."

The trading post in Keams Canyon was owned by members, and it had a café, and the missionaries were allowed to sign for a free meal once a week. It was always a treat. Often it was their bulwark against hunger. Sometimes it was the first real meal they'd had in a day or two. Coming to Keams Canyon was their favorite time of the week. The waitress was a Navajo woman in a Santa's hat who had been on placement up in Sandy when she was a girl, and her mother had gone to church years ago when she was a student at Intermountain Indian School in Brigham City, but each week she resisted the elders' suggestion that she come back to church.

"We'd love to see you there, Sister Yellowhair," Elder Taylor said.

But she was shy, or at least quiet, and said she was

busy on Sunday mornings and when she brought their drinks she also brought back the tip they'd left her the week before. She always did that. She gave them back their change and said it was the Lord's money and she didn't want to take it. She wanted them to have it. Which made Elder Hammon feel all the more guilty when he took four quarters and crossed the café to the jukebox and picked songs. It was always the same two songs. "Three Times a Lady" and "When I Need Love," old stuff, from Lionel Ritchie and Leo Sayer. He got six songs for a dollar, and that meant each song three times and then he would come back to the table and drink his lemonade and open his letters from home. Specifically his letters from girls back home. His lifeline.

"Look at this," he said to Elder Taylor, holding up a rectangle of coarse brown tissue. "This is what they use for toilet paper in Spain."

It was from a girl he'd met at a dance at BYU. One of those things where the women outnumber the men. There had been a group of four girls standing together that night, it was spring and outside, in some kind of a garden, and he had asked them all to dance. All at once. Like some group thing. Three had said yes and one had said no. So he danced with the three and thanked them and went to learn more about the fourth. She told him that if he wanted to dance with her, and with her alone, she would do it. She said she had no interest in a group dance, as that made no sense. She wasn't a child, she was a woman, and if she danced with a man it was because they were a man and a woman and perhaps a mutual interest might develop. That was the girl who'd sent the Spanish toilet paper. It was her first letter from the mission field, and she had sent him a souvenir.

"Look at this," Elder Hammon said, reaching for his Bible. "She sent me a scripture."

He flipped a few pages, to the third epistle of John, and put his finger under the second verse.

"Beloved," he read, "I wish above all things that thou mayest prosper and be in health, even as thy soul prospereth."

As they ate their salads, they debated back and forth the significance of the word "beloved." Elder Taylor teased and Elder Hammon hoped. She was quite a girl and she was everything but a good cook, and a year and a half to go was a very long time, especially for a young man who felt like he ought to be in love.

The tampiqueña was steak with enchilada sauce on it and Elder Hammon loved it. He sopped the surplus sauce up with his roll and nodded yes with a full mouth when the waitress asked if they were ready for pie, and as they began to eat that Elder Taylor asked him a question.

"What blessing do you think we're missing out on by listening to the jukebox?"

It wasn't a Pharisee question. Sometimes people will do that. Ask questions that are really condemnations. It was an honest question. It was a thought question.

"If we are blessed for our obedience," Elder Taylor said, "what blessing are we cheating ourselves out of by breaking that rule each week? If we're not supposed to listen to music, and we do listen to music, what portion of the Lord's help are we missing out on? How are we hurting ourselves and the people we teach?"

Elder Taylor liked the music, too. And he was a young man, too. And he wanted to be in love just as much as Elder Hammon did.

Elder Hammon put down his fork and looked up at Elder Taylor with a frown on his face. It wasn't anger, it was half thoughtfulness and half embarrassment.

"If you love me, keep my commandments," Elder Hammon said. "The degree to which we keep the commandments is a direct reflection of the degree to which we love the Lord."

"If we have trouble keeping the Lord's commandments," Elder Taylor said, "it is a sign we need to work on loving the Lord."

Together almost in unison they each began to quote, "There is a law irrevocably decreed in heaven . . ."

Then Elder Hammon extended his hand across the table and said, "Good point, elder. I'm done with the jukebox."

As Elder Taylor shook the outstretched hand he said, "It's funny, but there are guys out here who live the letter of the law but do it for the wrong reason. And there are guys out here who have goodness in their hearts but never quite learn obedience. I think doing the right thing is a combination of doing the right thing and doing it for the right reason.

"If we are to be disciples, we must be obedient. If we are to have all the Lord's blessings, we must be obedient. If we are to have integrity, we must be obedient. If we are to challenge people to live as the Lord asks them to live, we must live as the Lord asks us to live. If we teach people that the priesthood authority of God has been restored and that he speaks through his servants today, we must follow the counsel of those servants who have been put in authority over us. If we ask people to lose themselves in the service of God, we must lose ourselves in the service of God."

They finished their pie in silence, with Elder Hammon flipping his triple open to the fourth section of the Doctrine and Covenants, reading over it as he ate.

"It means she loves you," Elder Taylor finally said. "For crying out loud, she's a smart woman. She knows what 'beloved' means. She's telling you she loves you."

"How could she not?" Elder Hammon said. "I mean, let's be honest about this, I'm quite a catch."

Elder Taylor signed his name on the check the waitress had left and stood up and said loudly, "See you next week, Sister Yellowhair!" as he walked toward the door. Behind him, Elder Hammon quietly slipped some folding money beneath a plate at a booth in the corner the waitress had waited on but not yet cleared. On their table, the elders had left their remaining jukebox change and an old pamphlet from a box near the half-mouse-eaten gingerbread house in their trailer's back room. It was titled "What the Mormons Think of Christ."

Chapter Three

The Coochyumptewas missed church and canceled dinner, and the missionaries were nervous. They didn't know what Brother Coochyumptewa was thinking and they were afraid maybe things were going the wrong direction. To make things worse, Sister Jackson, who lived right next to the Sichomovi kiva, said Brother Coochyumptewa was in there almost every night. Elder Taylor called the president and told him that things weren't looking good and that he should tell the stake president that Brother Coochyumptewa might not be there Christmas Eve. The president had agreed that it did sound challenging but that he knew the Lord wanted Brother Coochyumptewa to be the branch president and that if the Lord wanted it then it was possible and they had to do everything they could to make it happen. The president said he would fast and he asked the elders to fast and with a week left till Christmas it was a time for faith, endurance and resourcefulness.

In Mormon pioneer times, much credence was given to the motto: The Lord helps those who help themselves. Brigham Young said that he didn't dare ask the Lord to do anything for him that he could do for himself, and Ezra Taft Benson said, "After making a request through prayer, we have a responsibility to assist in its being granted."

This is a roll-up-your-sleeves gospel, and the calling of a missionary is to work. Sure, there is praying and reading and pondering to be done, but preaching the gospel is primarily a calling of toil. The Lord sent his disciples out into the world to labor and counseled them in modern times to thrust in their sickles with their might. It's one of those things where if you're not tired, you're not doing it right. If it's not using up everything you have to give, you need to do it a little bit harder.

And you need to listen to the Spirit when it speaks.

Like it did the morning Elder Hammon was in the back room taking a picture of the gingerbread skeleton, the half-gone framework that was all that remained of the house that had come in the mail. The desert rats and mice were coming in in the night and gnawing the gingerbread and they had almost finished the task. As he knelt on the floor to take the picture he noticed behind the gingerbread house against the wall the old filmstrip projector missionaries had used years before. It caught his attention in an odd way, in a spiritual way, in that quick gush of thought or insight that is a spiritual prompting, and when he stood up he grabbed the projector and the box of filmstrips that sat beside it. Out at the table where they had companionship study, he opened and inspected the projector and Elder Taylor looked through the film-strips and their associated cassette tapes. Elder Hammon plugged the projector in and flicked on its fan and bright light and found them both to be operational.

"That's kind of cool," Elder Taylor said. "What are we going to do with it?"

"I don't know," Elder Hammon said, "but let's put it in the car. Let's take it with us."

That day they tracted Navajo hogans on the south-ern edge of the area, halfway to Winslow, because they'd never been down there, and in the afternoon they went up to Old Oraibi for singing practice with the kids. This was the last rehearsal before Christmas Eve and one of the mothers told the missionaries that she and some others had gotten green and red felt and were going to make bows for the girls and bow ties for the boys, to wear at the presentation. Though the elders had been out to Old Oraibi several times since their first visit, they had taken pains not to do much other than practice singing with the children and make friends with them. It was a display of patience, really, and an understanding that sometimes you have to wait until the right moment to make your move.

After practice the elders stopped at Shungopavi on

Second Mesa. A baby boy was sick there and the grandmother had called and asked for the elders to come bless him. She wasn't a member, but once, walking through the beautiful and ancient village, up on top of what seemed like a rock, they had seen her sitting in her doorway making a coil basket, and they had asked if they could watch. She had welcomed them and fed them lunch and showed them how she took a bundle of tiny willow shoots and wrapped it and wove it in a type of reed to make baskets and plaques that coiled outward, emblazoned with beautiful designs, for her family and to sell in Winslow. They had given her a Book of Mormon and half of a batch of cookies Elder Taylor's mother had sent and they stopped by whenever they were at Second Mesa and with the sick baby she wanted the elders to pray for him. So they explained to her about the priesthood and about faith and about how Jesus had sent his disciples out to heal the sick, and they lifted the baby up in their hands and in her little dirt-floor home they blessed it in the name of the Lord to be healed and strong.

It was early evening but dark when they got back to Polacca, and they decided to drive up on the mesa. There wasn't any particular reason, but as they came to the road they just both felt like going up. It didn't strike them any particular way, just that they thought they'd try to find some last thing to do before they went in for the night.

The kiva by the plaza in Sichomovi is a rectangular stone building with a ladder sticking out of the flat earthen roof. That is the only entrance. There are no windows and the kiva, like all kivas, sits partially underground. Inside, the kiva's one room is divided into two parts. One, against the rear wall, is raised six inches or a foot and comprises about a quarter or a third of the room's area. There are chairs, old surplus chairs from a school, in that portion. The rest of the room, sitting a little bit lower, is open. There is a small rectangular hole in the floor, usually covered over with wood. It is a special place through which the Hopis' gods can listen and watch what is happening in the kiva. Hanging from the log beams of the roof are strings, some dangling potsherds and others dangling the bones of birds.

That's where Brother Coochyumptewa was when the elders came onto the mesa.

They didn't know how they knew that, but they knew it. They felt it as a matter of fact, a certainty. And they felt that the Lord told them for a reason.

So they parked and decided to pray. A simple back-and-forth request for the Lord's guidance until they both felt sure of an answer. Elder Taylor prayed first and then Elder Hammon and then both of them again. And then they just sat there with their heads bowed and when after a few minutes they asked one another what they were thinking they both had focused on the filmstrip projector. The filmstrip projector and the cassette player and the kiva. And getting out of their car Elder Hammon grabbed the projector and Elder Taylor got the box of filmstrips and a stack of Jesus pictures and they walked over to Sister Jackson's house to ask if they could borrow her extension cord.

Ten minutes later they had the cord running out Sister Jackson's front door to a card table, in the center of the plaza next to the kiva, where they plugged in the film-strip projector and the cassette player. Elder Hammon flipped on the bright light, focused it against the stone wall of a house facing the plaza, and threaded "Man's Search For Happiness" behind the lens. Then he pushed Play on the cassette recorder and wheeled the volume up as high as it would go. A bit of dialog would be heard, then a beep, then more dialog. At each beep, the knob on the projector would need to be turned and the next picture would advance. The stillness of the plaza was overwhelmed by the sound track of the filmstrip. Almost immediately, people came to their doors and windows to see what was going on. Children were the first to run out and Elder Hammon quickly put one of them to work turning the knob at each beep. Soon people were carry-ing chairs out into the plaza, wrapped in sweaters and blankets, sitting down to watch the pictures projected on the wall. After "Man's Search for Happiness," Elder Hammon stood in front of the wall and welcomed them. Elder Taylor was changing filmstrips and, with the light off for a few minutes, cooling the bulb. Elder Hammon said they were missionaries from the Mormon Church—which everyone knew—and explained how the Mormon

Church came to be. When Elder Taylor gave him the sign, he introduced the next filmstrip—"Joseph Smith's First Vision"—and the show continued.

By the fourth filmstrip, there were probably a hundred people in the plaza, sitting or standing, watching the elders and their pictures. Between each film, the elders would give a short discussion. The First Vision, the Christmas story, the Word of Wisdom, and chastity. By then they were starting a series of filmstrips about a boy named Tom Trails. He was a Navajo who was sweet for a girl named Lilly and the people took quickly to his narrative.

And then something happened.

Men started climbing up the ladder out of the kiva. Curious about the noise, or irritated, the intended audience was coming. The men stood on top of the kiva for a couple of minutes, then sat on the edge of its roof, their feet dangling in the air, watching the films. In the dark Elder Taylor looked hard to see Brother Coochyumptewa.

After the third "Tom Trails," Elder Taylor took his turn addressing the crowd. He announced that there would be just one more filmstrip. That he would speak, and then the filmstrip, and then Elder Hammon would give a prayer. Then it would be time for the missionaries to leave. Also, they were all invited to a Christmas Eve program down at the church and the missionaries had a bunch of pictures of Jesus if anybody wanted one.

And then he began to speak.

"Brothers and sisters," Elder Taylor said, "other than the resurrection, there is just one miracle that is recorded in all four New Testament gospels. There was just one thing so big that Matthew, Mark, Luke and John each wrote about it. Do you know what it is?

"Well, I'll tell you. It's the feeding of the five thousand. You've heard the story, haven't you?

"Jesus and his apostles were in a desolate country, far from anyone's home. But people were so eager to see Jesus, and to hear him preach, that they had come into that wilderness with their families. The Bible says that there were five thousand men, plus their wives and children. It was a massive number of people, and Jesus and the apostles taught and blessed them all day. And then it was getting toward night and Jesus asked his disciples what they should do for dinner. One disciple said that Jesus should send the people home so they could get some food. Jesus said that they were too far from home. They talked about buying them food but there wasn't enough money and around there, there was nobody selling food.

"So Jesus asked them how much food they had with them. The disciples looked around and found out that from that whole mass of people, only one little boy had brought any food. And he had five loaves and two fishes. Probably, he had just enough for his own lunch and supper. Maybe his mom packed him some food, I don't know.

"But Jesus said to bring him the five loaves and two

fishes. And then you know what happened? Jesus blessed the food, and he broke it into pieces, and he gave it to the apostles to pass to the people. All of those five thousand men and their families had been sat down in groups and the Lord's followers passed that food out amongst them. And everybody ate all they wanted. And when they were done, there were twelve baskets of leftovers gathered up."

The people were silent. Most of them knew the story, but most of them did not know the enthusiasm and spirit of a Mormon missionary. They had heard or read the story before, but it was now being told to them by someone called and set apart to the task. This disciple of Christ was just like the disciples of Christ who had all those centuries ago passed the food to the people. This man spoke with authority, and with the Holy Ghost, which carried his words to the hearts of the humble and earnest before him, including those who sat on the edge of the kiva and dangled their legs.

"That's quite a miracle, isn't it?" Elder Taylor said. "But I've got a question.

"See, I believe the Lord does things for a reason. I believe he is always teaching us and trying to make us better and happier. And I think we should study and think about the things we read in the scriptures. So I have this question: Why did Jesus take all of the boy's food?

"Seriously. Why did the boy have to give up all of his food?

"Clearly, the Lord has the ability to take a finite

amount of food and bless it and turn it into an infinite amount of food. If the Lord could feed five thousand families with five loaves and two fishes, do you think he could have fed the same number of people with, say, three loaves and one fish? Don't you think? Probably, if he wanted to, he could have fed them all off one loaf and one fish. In fact, he could have fed them all off nothing—he did that for the children of Israel for forty years. Each morning they went outside their tent and there was manna. So in order to feed those five thousand families, Jesus didn't truly need to take all of that boy's food. He could have gotten the job done just as well with part of it and left the boy some for himself.

"But that's not the Lord's way. He's not interested in partial sacrifice. He's not interested in halfway. When the Lord calls us, he wants all of us. And you can't serve the Lord by holding back something for yourself. You're either all in, or you're not in. And the Lord took all that boy's lunch not because the Lord needed to take it all, but because the boy needed to give it all. If his sacrifice to the Lord was to mean anything, it had to be complete. He had to give everything he had.

"Now look at it this way. Can you feed five thousand men and their wives and children with five loaves and two fishes? No. You can't. At least you and I can't. So that little boy's offering, all alone, was inadequate. It wasn't enough. It wouldn't get the job done or come anywhere near close. But his offering, blessed by the Lord, became enough. It's the same way with us. We can be like that little boy. We just have to remember that we alone are inadequate. That what we have to offer is insufficient. But we still must offer it all. And when we give everything we have, and it is blessed by the Lord, it becomes miraculous, it becomes a tool in the Lord's hand.

"That's what we are called to do, brothers and sisters, we are called to be like that little boy. Others need us. Others are depending on us. And the Lord can use us. But we must give him everything that we are, and we must let him bless us and use us as he sees fit. That is the lesson of the feeding of the five thousand. Yes, the Lord can perform miracles. When he does, he typically uses people, people like you and me. But he uses us on his terms, not on ours, and if we are going to be his servants and followers, we must play by his rules.

"Now, brothers and sisters, you've been kind to listen to me. I am grateful. And I promise you, as a representative of Jesus Christ, that as you try to follow the Lord he will lead and guide you and bring you to him. I also tell you, as a representative of Jesus Christ, that he lives. That he is the very Son of God. That in a few days we will celebrate his birth in Bethlehem and that we will be commemorating something that truly happened. He was born, he was crucified, he was resurrected, and he lives today. I also testify to you that there is nothing—nothing—more important in this life than following him. I believe in him, and so do you. In your hearts right now you feel a warmth and an emotion that is the witness of the Holy Ghost to you that Jesus is the Christ and the Savior of us all. That feeling in your heart is the light for the path that leads back to the Lord. If you follow it, you will have peace in this life and the next. My companion and I have been sent to you to help you follow that light, and I hope you will let us do that."

Then he walked out of their sight and there was a moment of quiet, silent except for a scattering of sniffles, and then the bright light and the loud cassette and the next installment of "Tom Trails."

An hour later Elder Hammon pushed aside the curtain blocking off the back room and set the projector and the box of filmstrips behind what remained of the gingerbread house.

The morning of Christmas Eve the missionaries went out to Hotevilla on the far side of Third Mesa. It was a place where they still grew corn the old way and where in the warm season people walked through the drifting sand looking for the Hopi tea that tended to grow there. They would pick it as the small yellow flowers were coming on and then tie it into bundles to dry. The elders' trailer in Polacca had a drawer full of it and most mornings they dropped it in boiling water to warm them by the cupful.

They had gone to Hotevilla to make piki. More correctly, they had gone to Hotevilla because one of the ladies from church had an aunt in Hotevilla who had agreed to send some piki to the Christmas Eve social and she had said she didn't mind if the elders watched her make it.

She was a middle-aged woman who either didn't speak English or didn't want to speak English and though she was kind she wasn't conversant. They found her house OK and the first thing she did was gesture for them to cut some wood. Some fine-burning cedar. She wanted it cut and she wanted it cut small, into pieces she could feed into a fire with her hand. While Elder Taylor cut the wood, Elder Hammon watched the woman as she mixed hand-ground blue-corn meal in a big bowl with water and the ash of a certain plant. It made a smooth, purplish-blue batter. She tucked the big bowl under her arm and walked out to the piki house behind her home. It was a low building of rock and adobe, not tall enough to stand up in, and just barely big enough for the three of them to fit into. The interior was plastered smooth with a slip of mud, the hand prints of whoever had done the job still visible. It reminded Elder Taylor of a cliff dwelling he had explored on the Green River the summer before. It was a P-Day hike and they had climbed up to this cliff dwelling and inside found still intact the fine white slip with which the home had been plastered. Up in the corner, where the hand spreading the clay in broad arcs had been lifted away, there was a hand print with its fingerprints of whorls and ridges still perfectly visible. It had given him pause to see such a personal and individual sign of someone who had lived centuries before.

The Hopi lady gestured for Elder Taylor to bring the wood he had cut into the piki house and she kindled a fire with it beneath her piki stone. It was a rectangular black rock, flat and smooth and maybe an inch and a half thick. Its surface was almost polished and it sat horizontally on other stones and masonry that held it about a foot or a foot and a half off the floor. The Hopi lady sat on a block of stone so that her knees were almost against the edge of the piki stone. The piki house smelled strong of good cedar smoke. When the piki stone was hot enough, the lady stuck her hand in the blue-corn batter, cupping some in her palm, and lifted it onto the piki stone. In a rapid and graceful arc she swept her flat palm across the smooth face of the stone. The batter almost immediately cooked and dried and went grayish blue. She expertly rolled it on itself and quickly came with another cupping handful of batter which she likewise spread flat with the outer edge of her palm. As this turned papery she rolled it with the previous one and made a roll may be ten inches long and a couple or three inches in diameter that looked like an old blue parchment or papyrus. One after another she cupped and spread and rolled and cupped and spread and rolled and the piki house became a little humid and smelled of rich blue corn.

Periodically the Hopi woman would put more cedar into the fire beneath the piki stone and hand one or the other of the elders a plate stacked with piki to be carried into the house. When the batter was about half gone Elder Taylor pointed at it and the stone and indicated that he would like to try. The Hopi woman nodded consent and got up off the block and moved out of the way to make room for Elder Taylor. He sat on the block and folded his long legs out of the way and pulled the bowl of batter close beside him. Then he stuck his right hand into it, just as he had seen her do, cupping his hand slightly, bringing with it a little bit of batter, and he quickly moved it above the piki stone. Then, with a broad arcing sweep, he moved his hand across the surface of the piki stone, spreading the batter smoothly, as he had seen her do.

Except that, unlike her, he yelled. He almost screamed. A mixture of surprise and pain. He had just dragged his hand across a stone that was literally blistering hot.

And whereas she had a lifetime of tolerance and callus built up, his skin was tender and untried, and burned on the stone.

Laughing the way Hopi women laugh, the lady quickly urged him out of the piki house and pointed at the dog's water dish beside her home, indicating that he should put his hand in its cold contents to stop the burning. He did and she got him some ointment and a needle to pop the blisters and she had Band-Aids on him before she went back to finish her piki.

In another hour they were driving back across Hopi-land with four plates full of piki in the back seat.

⁂ Chapter Four

The missionaries were at the Polacca chapel two hours before the seven o'clock Christmas Eve program was to begin. They swept the cultural hall and got out a couple of folding tables and wiped them down clean and put Christmas wrapping paper on them for decoration and set out what refreshments they had. Various sisters in the branch had volunteered to bring more treats, and about an hour before people were to begin arriving the Relief Society president brought and set out a dozen plastic potted poinsettias around the chapel. The young men and young women had strung garlands of packing peanuts the Wednesday before and they were draped over the door and around the lectern. The branch clerk had printed up sheets of red and green paper with the lyrics to "Silent Night" and "O Little Town of Bethlehem." Brother Landry came up from the Polacca trading post with three of those big coolers construction workers hang off their trucks in the summertime. He mixed one with cherry drink, another with orange, and the third with grape.

The stake president got there about quarter to seven. He was a short and strong man, a rancher, a descendant of some of the pioneers sent down to colonize the Little Colorado. One side of his family was from Woodruff Butte and the other side was from Joseph City and his people had been in Indian country since it was all Indian country. He shook hands with the branch president and the missionaries and the Relief Society president and then sat in the back of the chapel, trying to stay out of the way. Shortly before seven the trucks began arriving from Old Oraibi. That had been one of the question marks. The children of Old Oraibi had taken immediately to the idea of coming to church on Christmas Eve, but nobody knew about the parents. As it turned out, they came and came and came. Parents and grandparents and aunts and uncles and people who didn't have any particular connection. The children all had on red and green felt bows. The boys around their necks and the girls in their hair. Each was wearing freshly pressed clothes, the best they had, and the missionaries pointed the children up onto the stand while their parents took a seat in the chapel pews. At a certain point the stake president stood up and opened the curtain that separated the chapel from the cultural hall and started setting up chairs for the overflow. A couple of fathers from Old Oraibi came and helped, along with a brother from the branch, and it took most of the stacked folding chairs before everyone arriving had a seat. The only other time they'd ever had to open that curtain was when the building was dedicated by Spencer W. Kimball and people came from as far away as Holbrook and Page to see an apostle in person.

At ten minutes after seven most of the people were in their seats and the Relief Society sisters had reorganized the snack tables and the Old Oraibi children were on the stand smiling brightly and waving to their parents.

All was set and ready. Everything except Brother Coochyumptewa. He had not come, and there was no indication that he would come, and there really wasn't any reason to delay any longer. Elder Taylor went to the branch president in his seat and whispered something to him. The branch president nodded and said something back. Then Elder Taylor went to the stake president, now on the back row of the folding chairs, and whispered something to him. The stake president patted him on the back and nodded and Elder Taylor walked to the front of the chapel, stepping up onto the dais past what would normally be the Sacrament table.

"Merry Christmas, brothers and sisters, and welcome," he said from the lectern. "We are so happy to have you here, and we want you to know that you are welcome, tonight and always.

"Tonight, together, we welcome our Savior, Jesus Christ, into the world. On this night we commemorate his birth, some two thousand years ago. We don't know what that night was like, we don't know when it was, but we know it happened. And we know that our loving Heavenly Father sent his Son to live and die for us, so that we could return and live with them both someday."

Then he introduced the branch president, to welcome the people, and the elders' quorum president, to give the opening prayer, and then Elder Hammon, to lead the children's choir.

Elder Hammon, of course, knew nothing about conducting music or leading a choir. But he and about three dozen of the youngsters of Old Oraibi knew plenty about singing for all they were worth. They had prepared five songs, all real Christmas songs, and they stood up and belted them out. The first was "Far, Far Away on Judea's Plains," written in St. George on a piano hauled across the Plains by Mormon pioneers. When that one was done, Elder Hammon had about a quarter of the children come one by one to the microphone and introduce themselves. As each said his or her name, various family groupings across the chapel beamed and buzzed. Then it was "Hark! The Herald Angels Sing," and another quarter of the children at the lectern and "Oh, Come, All Ye Faithful" and another quarter of the children and then "O Little Town of Bethlehem" with the audience standing and joining in after the first verse. The final group of children was introduced and then they sang "Silent Night" with the audience also joining in after the first verse. Some of the parents were teary eyed and all of the parents were happy and the children almost glowed.

Then Brother Funk walked to the dais and without introduction began reading from Luke chapter 2. He had a kind, loving, fatherly voice and the words sounded beautiful as he read them. He explained why Jesus had to be born and why there had to be a Savior. He talked about the times we lived in and the times Jesus lived in. He explained that there were people living in the Americas when Jesus was born, and that they knew of and had been looking forward to his birth. He said that they all had been watching, all of them in that room, when Jesus had been born, and that they were part of the heavenly host that had shouted, "Glory to God in the highest, and on earth peace, good will toward men." He told them that they had been Jesus' followers before they were born, and he was calling them all to be his followers now.

That's when Elder Taylor heard the slightest little sob. From the back of the cultural hall. Near the rear exit. Looking back he saw the stake president standing next to a man, with his arm around his shoulders. It was Brother Coochyumptewa. He had come in the back door and the stake president was standing beside him and the stake president had his arm around his shoulders as he cried.

Brother Funk said that Jesus didn't want gold, frankincense, and myrrh. He wanted our hearts. He wanted us to give him our promise and our lives. He wanted us to live the way he asked us to live. Not to enslave us, but to free us. He said that Jesus knew pain and sorrow and knew how to comfort us in our pain and sorrow, and, most importantly, he knew how to free us from our pain and sorrow. Then Brother Funk bore his testimony of Jesus and said that he knew he lived and was the Son of God, just as assuredly as if he'd met him on the street and shaken his hand. Then he invited Sister Funk up and the two of them sang, "I Know That My Redeemer Lives." When the song was over they silently returned to their seats.

Elder Taylor walked to the lectern and thanked everyone for coming. He thanked the children of Old Oraibi for their wonderful music. He thanked the Funks for singing and Brother Funk for speaking. He said that the meeting would close with a prayer offered by the Relief Society president and that after that there would be refreshments and socializing. He said that there would be new piki, and, holding up his burned hand, he said that he had helped make it. The Hopis in the audience giggled and looked at him fondly.

"But before the prayer," Elder Taylor said, "we will hear from our concluding speaker—Brother Coochyumptewa."

As he walked off the dais he uttered a silent prayer that Brother Coochyumptewa would walk forward.

And he did. Slowly. Slowly and humbly. He quietly walked to the front and took his position. Not shy, but modest. A simple salt-of-the-earth man standing behind a lectern with three rows of children behind him and his future in front of him.

"For all of my life Jesus has been carrying my sins on him. For all my life, when I've done wrong, it's been him who's had to pay. He's been carrying me. But for all my life, I haven't done anything for him. I've always done for me. I've always done what I wanted, what I thought would make me happy. But none of it did. None of it made me happy. Because none of it was for him. I've been living a selfish life, a faithless life, and that's not a happy life.

"In the Bible there is a guy, and he was just going somewhere, and when they were going to kill Jesus they got this guy and they made him carry Jesus' cross. That's who I want to be. I want to be the guy who carries Jesus' cross. I can't keep him from being crucified. I can't keep him from suffering. But if I can do one little thing to help him, I want to. I want to do that. But when you are carrying Jesus' cross, you can't carry anybody else's cross. You can only carry one load. That's all you can do. And if there are other crosses there, you've got to decide which one you're going to carry.

"So I want you to know, with all my heart, I believe in Jesus Christ. He is my Savior. He is my Elder Brother. He is the Son of God. And I carry his cross.

"Nothing else is more important. Nothing else deserves my loyalty. Nothing else has a piece of my heart. And if I have to give up everything in order to gain eternal life, I will do it. I am, to the core of my being, a follower of Jesus Christ, everything else comes second, and some things simply cannot be."

"Jesus Christ bought me with his Atonement. I am his. And I am going to act like I am his. I am going to live a Christ-centered life. You can count on me, and so can the Lord."

And then he sat down, and the meeting concluded as planned. And the cultural hall was soon full of happy children and their parents, the missionaries going among them shaking hands and introducing themselves, the people of Old Oraibi making the acquaintance of the people of the Polacca Branch, shared greetings of "Merry Christmas" on every lip. From family to family the elders went, asking if they could come and discuss the things Brother Funk and Brother Coochyumptewa had spoken about, taking down names and making appointments. The Primary president and the people who worked with the Young Women and Young Men told the parents and children about classes and activities and together they ate finger sandwiches and cookies and piki. A full hour after the program ended there were still some who lingered and talked. The fathers of Old Oraibi had long since put up the chairs and a couple of their sons pushed the big brooms back and forth across the cultural hall floor while their mothers and the Relief Society ladies cleaned up the food and washed the dishes that needed it. While down the hall in an office the stake president spoke first to Brother Coochyumptewa and then to Brother

Coochyumptewa and his wife. All three walked out of the office with smiles and tears.

And a half an hour later still the missionaries walked out of the now-darkened church, crossing the gravel lot to their trailer.

"This is why I came on a mission," Elder Hammon said. "This was the best night. I am so grateful to be here, so thankful to be a part of this work. I am so glad I'm in Hopiland."

"And get this," Elder Taylor said, "tomorrow you get to call home."

"That's right," Elder Hammon said. "I forgot. It'll be my first call home since I came out. I can't wait to tell my family about tonight. They'll so wish they were here. They'll so wish they were on a mission."

"Maybe so, my friend," Elder Taylor said. "At any rate, they'll be glad you're on a mission. Completely on a mission. They'll be proud of you. And they ought to be."

Elder Hammon looked at him. He was struck by the compliment, and suddenly by the change in himself.

"Merry Christmas, Elder Taylor," he said.

"Merry Christmas, Elder Hammon," came the response.

Inside they had prayer and went to bed, falling quickly asleep. In the junk room the last of the gingerbread house was gone. All that was left were some crumbs and hard candies and a few sticks of stale licorice.

About the Author

BOB LONSBERRY is a radio talk show host who has worked as a newspaper columnist and reporter. He served as a missionary for The Church of Jesus Christ of Latter-day Saints on and around the Indian reservations of the American Southwest.

A decorated veteran of the U.S. Army, he lives in Mount Morris, New York, which is the birthplace of Francis Bellamy, the author of the Pledge of Allegiance. He is married and is the father of six children.